IRISH PROVERBS

IRISH
Proverbs

FIONNUALA WILLIAMS

POOLBEG

First published 1992 by
Poolbeg Press Ld
Knocksedan House,
Swords, Co Dublin, Ireland

© Compilation Fionnuala Williams, 1992

The moral right of the author has been asserted.

ISBN 1 85371 154 3

Cover design by Pomphrey Associates
Set by Richard Parfrey in Stone Serif
Printed by The Guernsey Press Company Ltd,
Vale, Guernsey, Channel Islands

In fond memory of my mother Rosemary Moon Carson.

The heaviest ear of corn bends the lowest.
Is í an dias is troime is ísle a choras a ceann.

CONTENTS

PREFACE

Although the following pieces of traditional advice—in the form of proverbs—were collected over fifty years ago, many are still used today. This is because relevant proverbs survive the generations if their message continues to be appropriate to the new era. Sometimes the format stays the same and sometimes it varies to suit new ideas and conditions.

Most of the proverbs found in Ireland can also be found in various languages throughout many other countries of Europe. This shows that we share a common cultural heritage. Proverbs have a complex history and each would need to be studied individually to be certain of its ancestry. In Ireland there are many which were first used exclusively in Irish and came to have English versions only in recent times; there are also those which were first used in English and then adopted into Irish, and then there are some which never passed into the other language.

Ireland's long literary history has also played its part in moulding its proverbs, for example in the style known as the triad in which three things are grouped—

> Three things that are labour in vain:
> throwing water on a drowned mouse,
> whistling jigs to a milestone in the expectation of a dance
> and ringing pigs in frosty weather.

This type of proverb was developed extensively in Irish literature and it is certainly partly because of this that the style has continued in use in the proverbs of the oral tradition until the present century.

The selection in this volume was made from proverbs collected from oral tradition in the English language. Most of them have no obvious contemporary equivalents in England and the rest vary from the standard English. Naturally in Ireland the proverbs in both English and Irish enjoy a close relationship with each other and many of those found in one language can also be found in the other. Irish language versions are given under the English. Many proverbs are mirrored exactly in the two languages, while some vary and others still appear to have no version in Irish.

The repertoire of proverbs used by any particular community reflects its concerns and attitudes, and many of them draw their metaphors from everyday life. For this book I have purposely chosen proverbs which will give a flavour of traditional rural life, where the images are taken from hearth and farm rather than from further afield.

ACKNOWLEDGEMENTS
AND NOTES

The English language proverbs in this book are published
with the kind permission of Professor Bo Almqvist, Head of
the Department of Irish Folklore, University College, Dublin.
They form part of the Schools' Manuscripts Collection which
dates to the late 1930s. The proverbs were collected from
oral tradition. This is the first time that a substantial number
of them have appeared in print. They are given largely as
in the original manuscripts with only a few minor
adjustments to punctuation and spelling.

The Irish language proverbs are reprinted with the kind
permission of An Gúm, Brainse na bhFoilseachán den
Roinn Oideachais. They are from the three main published
collections of proverbs from oral tradition [see below]; new
editions of two of these are in print. They cover a wider
time span than those in English: the majority belong to
the first four decades of this century but a few spread back
over the second half of the last. If a version exactly the

same as the English occurred in Irish this is given; if not then the next closest. Occasionally a different proverb which expresses a similar sentiment has been included when a similar version of the original proverb was not evident. These proverbs in Irish are indicated by an asterisk.

As any proverb can be applied in a variety of situations the proverbs here have been loosely arranged according to the scenes which they depict, such as butter-making, sheep rearing, markets and so on, rather than according to meaning. Sometimes several variants have been listed together.

The three main published collections are:

Énrí Ó Muirgheasa, Editor, *Seanfhocail Uladh* [Proverbs of Ulster]; new edition edited by Nollaig Ó hUrmoltaigh, Oifig an tSoláthair, Baile Átha Cliath 1976. The original was published in 1906.

An Seabhac, Editor, *Seanfhocail na Mumhan* [Proverbs of Munster]; new edition edited by Pádraig Ua Maoileoin, An Gúm, Baile Átha Cliath 1984. The original was published in 1926.

Tomás S Ó Máille, Editor, *Sean-Fhocla Chonnacht* [Proverbs of Connaught] Oifig an tSoláthair, Baile Átha Cliath; Iml. 1, 1948, Iml. 2, 1952.

In the text that follows, the collection from which the Irish version of the proverb is taken is indicated by the letter [U] for *Seanfhocail Uladh*; [M] for *Seanfhochail na Mumhan*; and [C] for *Sean-Fhocla Chonnacht*. Because there has been no new edition of *Sean-Fhocla Chonnacht*, the spelling of the proverbs from this collection has been modernised.

FIRESIDE
AND
CANDLELIGHT

"What harm?" says Jerry when he burned the house.

•

A man's house is his castle.

•

It's a poor house that can't keep one lady.

•

Keep your house and your house will keep you.
Coinnigh do shiopa is coinneoidh do shiopa thú. [C]

•

A house divided will soon fall.
Nuair bhíos daoine i bpáirt bíonn cuid ar leith is coimhlint. [C]*

•

It is easier to knock a house than to build one.

•

There's no corner like one's own corner.
There is no hearthstone like your own hearthstone.
Níl aon teallach mar do theallach féin. [C]

•

Home sweet home and the fire out.

Bare walls make giddy housekeepers.
Ballaí fuara a níos bean tí suarach. [C]

•

A red chimney, a hot house.

•

When everybody's house is on fire go home and look at your own chimney.
Nuair atá teach do chomharsan le thine tabhair aire do do theach féin. [U]

•

It is easier to build two chimneys than to keep smoke in one.

•

It takes a dirty hand to make a clean hearth.

•

It is easy to kindle a fire on an old hearth.
It is never hard to light a half-burned turf.
Is furas aibhleog a fhadú. [U]

•

A spark may raise an awful blaze.
Is beag an aithinne a dhéanfadh dó. [C]

•

Kindle the dry sticks and the green ones will catch.

•

Little sticks kindle a fire, great ones put it out.

•

Ash green makes a fire for the queen.

A little fire to warm you is better than a great one to harm you.

Is fearr tine bheag a ghoras ná tine mhór a loisceas. [U]

•

Don't burn your fingers when you have a tongs.

•

Silk stockings and burned shins.

Is minic a bhíos stocaí bána ar shála dóite. [C]

Stocaí bána ar loirgne breaca. [C]

•

The hag is the better of being warmed but she is worse of being burned.

Is fearrde dhon chailleach a goradh, ach is miste dhi í a loscadh. [C]

•

It's often the ashy pet put out the man that makes the stack.

Chuir fear na luatha fear na cruaiche amach. [M]

• • •

"More light," said the hag when the house was on fire.

"More light," arsa an chailleach nuair a bhí an teach le thine. [U]

•

Never burn a penny candle looking for a halfpenny.

•

When you burn the candle you can burn the butt.

Burn the candle and burn the inch.

Nuair a chaith tú an choinneal, caith an t-orlach. [U]

When the two ends are alight the candle does not burn long.

Nuair atá dhá thaobh na coinnle lasta, cha seasann sí i bhfad. [U]

•

The man in the moon wants no peeled rushes.

[Peeled rushes were used in the making of rush lights. Rushes were stripped to expose the pith which was then dried and dipped in melted fat to form slender candles.]

• • •

Dull tins, lazy housekeeper.

•

Sweep the corners—the middle will sweep itself.

•

A new broom sweeps clean but the old one knows the corners best.

Scuabann scuab úr go glan, ach tá fios ag an seanscuab ar na coirnéil. [U]

•

Sit on your heels till the stool is footed.

Ná suigh ar an stól go mbí sé formáilte fút. [C]

•

Don't break your *laidhricín* on a stool that isn't in your way.

[*Laidhricín* (Irish) means little toe; the proverb was collected in County Sligo.]

Ná bris do lorgain ar stól nach bhfuil in do shlí. [C]

You can't make a mahogany table out of a whin bush.

•

You can't make a piano out of a bacon box.

•

Never bolt your door with a boiled carrot.

•

Many feathers make a bed.

•

There is no place like the bed.
Níl áit ar bith mar an baile. [C]

•

He's a very drunk man that would fall out of a settle bed.
[A settle bed was the forerunner of the bed-settee; when it was
opened out into a bed it had high box-like sides.]

•

The drop follows the scollop.
[In heavy rain the water often ran in along the scollops, also
called scallops—the sally rods which were used in many areas to
secure the roof thatch. The proverb has been used to describe
how a certain family characteristic will descend through several
generations.]

•

A windy day is not the day for the scollops.
Chan é lá na gaoithe lá na scolbach. [U]
It's useless cutting scallops when the wind rises.
It is too late to point the scallops when the wind rises.

•

An empty house needs no thatch.
Scioból folamh, cha bhíonn díon de dhíth air. [U]

— 7 —

It is a lonesome street without a cart.

[This proverb was collected in County Leitrim, an area where street can mean farmyard.]

Is uaigneach an rud teach folamh. [C]

TENANTS
AND
LANDLORDS

Dunkles rising and castles falling.
[Dunkle is possibly a local word for dunghill or midden]
Tá na caisleáin ag titim is na cairn aoiligh ag éirí. [C]

•

There is many a slippy stone at a gentleman's hall door.
Is lúfar leac ag doras na huaisle. [U]

•

It is not the big mansion that makes the happy home.

•

An empty house is better than a bad tenant.
Is fearr teach folamh ná drochthionónta. [U]

•

Cleaning the house will not pay the rent.
Ní teach glan a íocfas cíos. [C]

•

Rent for the landlord or food for the children.
Said when someone was having difficulty in apportioning money
and also found in the following even more forthright form:
Your lord's rent or your child's life.
Cíos do thiarna nó bia do linbh. [C]

Many a baron wore a *báinín* (bawneen).

[Bawneen (Irish *báinín*) is a homespun white cloth.]

•

Three removes are worse than an eviction.

[Removing or flitting was generally not approved of. This is an adaptation of the following more widely known proverb which refers to fires]

Two removes are as bad as a burning.

•

Pay Leitrim the rent and you're safe.

[This was collected in County Leitrim, the Lords Leitrim having been major landlords there.]

FOOD
AND
DRINKS

"My belly thinks my throat is cut," as the hungry man said.

Síleann mo bholg go bhfuil mo scornach gearrtha. [U]

•

A hungry eye sees far.

Is géar súil an duine ocraigh. [U]

•

Hunger is good kitchen.

Is maith an t-anlann an t-ocras. [U]

Hunger is a good sauce, if it doesn't choke you it will fatten you.

•

Hunger will conquer a lion.

•

It is a good thing to be hungry when you have something to eat.

•

Where there is a gant there is a want [for meat, money or drink].

[Gant means a yawn or gape in Scots.]

Talk doesn't fill the stomach.
Cha líontar an bolg le caint. [U]

•

As is the cook so is the kitchen.

•

A blunt knife shows a bad housekeeper.

•

A good fire makes a speedy cook.
Ní tine mhaith cócaire tapaidh. [U]

•

What won't choke will fatten and clean dirt is no poison.

•

The worst at work is first at the table.
Fear ag an bhia is dearóil san obair. [U]
Last to the work, first to the table.
Tús ag an phota is deireadh ag an obair. [U]

•

Help is always welcome except at the table.
Is maith an rud cúnamh, ach ag an mbord. [C]

•

Easy to be *flaithiúil* with another person's share.
[Flaithiúil (Irish) means generous.]
Nach flaithiúil atá tú fá chuid do chomharsan? [C]

•

Don't put in your cutty among spoons.
[Don't meddle. Cutty here is most likely a short-handled horn spoon.]
Ná cuir do ladar i meadar gan iarraidh. [C]

•

You don't know what is in the pot till the lid is lifted.

Cool before you sup.
Fuaraigh sula n-óla tú. [U]

•

A fat kitchen never leaves a lean will.

•

A little tastes sweet.
Bíonn blas ar an bheagán. [U]

•

A fat kitchen makes a lean purse.

•

A full stomach never thinks of an empty one.
Cha dtuigeann bró sháitheach bró thámhach. [U]

•

Don't leave a tailor's remnant behind you.
Ná fág fuíollach táilliúir in do dhiaidh. [U]

•

Scant feeding to man or horse is a small profit and sure loss.

•

He sups ill, who eats all at dinner.

•

One without dinner means two for supper.
Duine gan dinnéar beirt chun suipéir. [M]

BUTTER AND BUTTER-MAKING

Before creameries became widespread every house had its churn and in season butter making was practically an everyday activity. Good butter was prized and what was not needed at home could be marketed.

A running cow's milk is hard to churn.

•

Long churning makes bad butter.
Maistreadh fada a níos an drochim. [U]
The longer the churning the tougher the butter.
A long churning makes bad butter, but be sure and have the churn scrubbed.

•

The more water the less butter.

•

Some people, when they get their heads above the churn, would not drink buttermilk.

•

Winded butter tastes bad.

•

Yellow butter sells best.

•

The person who has butter gets more butter.
Té a bhfuil im aige gheibh sé im. [U]
A variation on the more frequent:
They who have much get more.
An té a bhfuil mórán aige, is é a gheibh. [U]

Butter won't choke a dog.
Is iomaí caoi le cat a thachtadh seachas a thachtadh le him.
[C]
Don't buy butter for cats to lick.

•

It's dear bought butter that's licked off a briar.
An té arb ansa leis mil as neantóig, íocann sé ródhaor as. [C]

•

Butter to butter is no kitchen.
Im le him chan tarsann é. [U]
Champ to champ will choke you.
[Kitchen means relish—a little dab of something well-flavoured added to plain fare to make it more appetising. Champ is a Northern name for mashed potatoes. The proverb has been used when two men are seen dancing together or when two women kiss.]

•

Never put the butter through the porridge.
The butter will burst through the stirabout.
[Stirabout is an alternative name for porridge.]

•

The butter went through the colcannon on him.
D'imigh an t-im tríd an chál cheannann air. [U]
[This means that his plans miscarried. Colcannon was a popular dish of mashed potato mixed with chopped vegetable such as cabbage and onion.]

MEAL AND PORRIDGE

If you don't save at the cord you can't do it at the bottom.
I mbéal an mhála a bhíonn an bhainistí. [M]
Always going to the chest and never putting in soon brings
the meal to the bottom.

•

You can't make stirabout without meal.
Cha dtig leat leite a dhéanamh gan min. [U]
It's hard to make stirabout without meal.
Is deacair brachán a dhéanamh gan min. [C]

•

Half and half makes good porridge.
[That is, a mixture of half corn to half Indian meal. At one time
corn was so dear to buy that it was mixed with the cheaper
Indian meal to make it go further.]

•

There is skill in all things even in making porridge.

•

Nature binds the meal to the potstick.

•

Where there's meal there is surely salt.

•

Don't put in your spoon where there is no porridge.

•

Don't scald your lips with another man's porridge.

BREAD

It is easy to bake beside the meal.
Is furas fuineadh in aice mine. [U]

•

A man who has a loaf will get a knife to cut it.
An té a bhfuil builín aige, gheobhaidh sé scian a ghearrfas é. [C]

•

A slice off half a loaf is not missed.

•

Crooked bread makes straight bellies.
Ní arán cam bolg díreach. [U]

•

Raw dods make fat lads.
[A dod is a kind of bread.]

BROTH, MEAT AND VEGETABLES

You cannot sup soup with a fork.
Níl ann ach seafóid a bheith ag ól anraithe le forc. [C]

•

The second boiled broth is always the best.

•

Keep your heart up for frettin's but bad kitchen to your meat.
Coinnigh suas do chroí, beidh aimsir mhaith againn go sea. [U]

•

A stew boiled is a stew spoiled.

A bit of a rabbit is worth two bits of a cat.
Is fearr greim de choinín ná dhá ghreim de chat. [U]

•

"Just to have it to say," said the old man who ate the bit of the dog.

•

A pig's ear can never make mutton.

•

Chicken today and feathers tomorrow.

•

The younger the chicken the sweeter the picking.

•

An egg today is better than a roasted ox tomorrow.
Is fearr ubh inniu ná damh amárach. [C]

•

A good apple-eater is a bad sharer.

•

Some likes an apple and some likes an onion.

•

The old man to the big potato.

•

Better have potatoes and salt—and peace.

MILK AND TEA, WATER, WINE AND PORTER

The juice of a cow is good alive or dead.
Is maith sú bó, beo nó marbh. [U]

•

No cure for spilled milk only lick the pitcher.
Níl aon fháil ar an mbainne a doirtear. [C]

•

Don't skim the top off the milk before you send it to the creamery.

•

Tea seldom spoils when water boils.

•

Dead with tea and dead without it.
Marbh le tae agus marbh gan é. [U]

•

There is nothing as mean as tea in a tin.

•

He who only drinks water does not get drunk.
An té a ólas ach uisce, cha bhíonn sé ar meisce. [U]

•

Water is a good drink if taken in the right spirit.

•

Wine today, water tomorrow.
Fíon inniu, uisce amárach. [C]

•

Wine drowns more men than water.

•

Wine is sweet but the results are bitter.

The three faults of drink is:
a sorrowful morning,
a dirty coat
and an empty pocket.
Trí bhua an ólacháin:
maidin bhrónach,
cóta salach,
pócaí folamha. [C]

•

The drunkard will soon have daylight in through the rafters.
An té a leanas ól, chan fada go dtiocfaidh solas an lae isteach
ar mhullach an toighe. [U]

•

Except you are drinking never lean against a public house.
Ach mur' mbeidh tú ag ól, ná bí ag cuimil do dhroma don toigh
leanna. [U]

•

You'll never miss the porter until the barrel runs dry.
A parody of the more widely known:
You'll never miss the water till the well runs dry.
Níl fhios cén scáth atá sa tom go ngearrfar í. [C]

•

Empty kettles never leak.

FARM ANIMALS

ASSES AND HORSES

What would you expect from an ass but a kick?
Cad é bheadh súil agat a fháil ó bhó ach preab? [U]

●

An empty ass keeps his kicking end down.

●

Put an ass to grass and he will come home an ass.
Asal is ea asal pé'r bith áit a mbíonn. [C]

●

An ass never goes bald.

●

I cannot whistle, chew meal and drive an ass.
Cha dtig le duine feadalaigh agus min a chogaint. [U]
Ní féidir bheith ag seoladh na mbó is dá mbleán. [U]

●

Slow but sure like Murphy's ass.

●

Better is an ass that carries you than a horse that throws
you.
Is fearr asal a iomchras thú ná capall a chaitheas thú. [U]

A whip for the horse,
a bridle for the donkey
and a rod for the fool's back.
Bó le bata is capall le ceansacht. [M]

●

Better a poor horse in an empty stall, better half a loaf than
none at all.
Is fearr leathbhuilín ná bheith folamh ar fad. [U]

●

Those who would slight my horse would buy my horse.
An fear a cháineas mo ghearrán, ceannóidh sé mo ghearrán. [U

●

You can't judge a horse by his harness.

●

Saddle the right horse.
Cuir an diallait ar an chapall cheart. [U]

●

Some for the saddle and more for the straddle.
[Some for lighter work than others. A straddle is a pack saddle
from which panniers were hung. It was once widely used on
both horses and donkeys.]

●

A grey horse looks well in a bog.
Is furas gearrán bán a fheiceáil ar an chorrach. [U]

●

The best horse jumps the ditch.
An capall is fearr, léimfidh sé an claí. [U]

●

He's a good horse that pulls his own load.
Is maith an capall a tharraingeos a hualach féin. [C]

It is a proud horse won't carry his own corn.
Gan fhónamh an capall nach n-iompródh a choirce féin. [U]

•

An eating horse won't founder.

•

An old horse needs fresh grass.

•

It's hard to put an old horse from kicking.
Is deacair falaireacht a bhaint as seanchapall. [U]

•

A borrowed horse has hard hooves, *or* has no soul.
Bíonn cosa cruaidh ag gearrán iasacht'. [U]

•

It is easy to drive with your own whip and another's horse.
Do fhuip féin is capall na comharsan. [C]

COWS

The man of the cow in the tail.
Fear na bó 'san ruball. [U]

•

The worst cow in the bawn bawls first.
[Bawn—cattle-fold.]

•

"Every man to his fancy, and me to my own Nancy," said
the old woman when she kissed her cow.

•

The taste of the clover makes a thief of the cow.

The old cow for the sour grass.
[Sour grass is coarse grass.]

•

From her head the cow is milked.
Is as a ceann a bhlítear an bhó. [U]

•

A starved cow never fills the pail.

•

I'd far rather the cow that would give the full of a thimble than the one that would give the full of a churn and spill it.
B'fhearr gabhar nach dtabharfadh ach lán méaragáin ná bó a bhéarfadh lán na cuinneoige is a dhoirtfeadh. [U]
What is the use of a good cow when she spills her milk?
Cén mhaith bó mhaith, dá ndoirteadh sí a cuid bainne? [U]

•

Modest maoly the biggest devil in the byre.
[Maoly (Irish *maolaí*) cattle are a hornless breed peculiar to Ireland, only a small number of which still exist. The proverb may be referring to this type, or simply to a dehorned cow.]
An mhart mhodhúil mhaol an mhart is crosta i dteach na mbó. [U]

•

A bad cow is better than none.
Is fearr buaile seasc ná buaile folamh. [M]

•

A heifer's heifer fills the byre.

There are long horns on the cows in Connaught.
Tá adharca fada ar bhuaibh i gConnachta. [U]
Kerry cows have long horns.
Cows in Meath have long horns.
[The English versions above all came from County Cavan. Place-names are rarely mentioned in Irish versions.]
Cows across the sea have long horns.
Bíonn adharca fada ar na ba thar lear. [C]
Faraway cows have long horns but they often come home mileys.
[Mileys has the same meaning as maoly (see above) which means hornless.]

•

No cow no care no errand to the fair.

SHEEP AND GOATS

Tethered sheep will not thrive.

•

Do not loose the sheep for a halfpenny worth of tar.
Ná caill an chaora fá luach leithphingine tharra. [U]

•

Every scabby sheep likes a comrade.
Cha raibh caora chlamhach ar an tréad riamh nár mhaith léi comrádaí a bheith aici. [U]

•

One scabby sheep spoils a whole flock.
Salachaidh aon chaora chlamhach sréad. [U]

If one sheep puts his head through the gap the rest will follow.

An rud a níos gabhar déanfaidh gabhar eile é. [C]

Nuair a chacann gé cacann siad go léir. [M]

Nuair a luíonn gé luíonn siad go léir. [M]

•

Like and alike is a bad mark among sheep.

Cosúil le chéile—sin drochmharc i measc na gcaorach. [U]

•

Don't go putting wool on the sheep's back.

Is dona an rud an iomarca saille a chur ar dhroim muice beathaithe. [C]

•

"You're a devil, my dear," says Ned Ennis to the goat.

•

When you see a goat you should always hit him because he is either going into mischief or coming out of it.

•

When the goat goes to the door of the chapel she will not stop until she goes to the altar.

Nuair a théann an gabhar 'on teampall ní stadann go haltóir. [M]

•

If you put a silk suit on a goat it is still a goat.

Cuir síoda ar ghabhar is is gabhar i gcónaí é. [U]

•

It is difficult to cut wool off a goat.

Olann a bhaint de ghabhar nó iarraidh abhrais ar phocán. [M]

Riding on a goat is better than the best of walking.
Is fearr marcaíocht ar ghabhar ná coisíocht ar fheabhas. [U]

PIGS

A full pig in the sty doesn't find the hungry one going by.
Ní aithníonn an mhuc a bhíos sa chró an mhuc a bhíos ag dul an ród. [U]

•

It's a young pig that wouldn't hoke.
[Hoke means to root.]

•

It is not the big sow that eats the most.
Na muca ciúine a itheann an mhin. [M]

•

Pigs won't thrive on clean water.

•

The thieving pig's ear can hear the grass growing.
Éisteacht na muice bradaí.
D'aireodh sé an féar ag fás. [M]

DOGS AND CATS

What could you expect from a dog but a bite?

•

You cannot trust a cur.

•

For a mischievous dog a heavy clog.

Throw a bad dog a bone—a good dog won't bite you.
Caith an cnámh chuig an drochmhada 's ní baol duit an dea-mhada. [C]

•

A well-bred dog goes out when he sees them preparing to kick him out.

•

It's hard to make a choice between two blind dogs.
Is deacair rogha a bhaint as dhá ghabhar chaocha. [M]

•

Idle dogs worry sheep.

•

The dog is teann at his own door.
[*Teann* (Irish) means bold or confident.]
Is teann an madadh ar a thairseach féin. [U]

•

A dog with two homes is never any good.

•

Don't let your bone go with the dog.
Ná lig do chnámh leis an mada. [C]

•

Keep the bone and the dog will follow.
Coinnigh an cnámh agus leanfaidh an madadh thú. [U]

•

The dog that fetches will carry.

•

Every dog has its duties.

•

Every dog has his day and some have two.

The old dog for the hard road and the pup for the boreen.
[Boreen (Irish *bóithrín*) means a small road or lane or track]
*An seanmhada dhon bhealach fada, is an coileán le haghaidh
an bhóithrín.* [C]

•

It's hard to knock an old dog off his track.
Is deacair an mada a bhaint den tseanchasán. [C]

•

An old dog cannot alter his way of barking.

•

To steal an old dog never try you'll find your mistake by
and by.

•

It's hard to teach an old dog to dance.
Is deacair damhsa a chur roimh sheanmhadadh. [U]

•

You should not throw stones at a dead dog.
Caitheamh cloch ar mhadadh marbh. [U]

•

A dead dog will not bark.

•

If the cat scrape you don't beat the dog.

•

"I saw you before," says the cat to the boiling water.
*"Chonac cheana thú," mar a dúirt an cat leis an mbainne
beirithe.* [M]

•

Would a cat drink sweet milk?
An maith leis an gcat bainne leamhnachta? [U]

If the cat was churning it is often she would have her paws in it.

Dá mbeadh cuigeann ag an gcat ba mhinic a lapa féin ann. [M]

•

A wise cat never burned herself.

Níor dhóigh seanchat riamh é féin. [M]

•

One jump in the fire never burnt the cat.

•

What the good wife spares the cat eats.

An rud a choigleas na mná, itheann an cat é. [U]

•

Too many cats are worse than rats.

•

If the cat sits long enough at the hole she will catch the mouse.

•

When the cat is out the mouse can dance.

Nuair bhíos an cat amuigh, bíonn cead rince ag na luchóga. [C]

•

The cat's one shift is worth all the fox's.

•

The cat has leave to look at the queen and the queen has leave to shoot it.

Tá cead ag an gcat breathnú ar an mbanríon. [C]

Tá cead ag an gcat breathnú ar an rí, is tá cead ag an rí é a chaitheamh. [C]

A cat purrs for himself.

Ar mhaithe leis féin a dheineann an cat crónán. [M]

It isn't for nothing the cat winks when she shuts both her eyes.

•

Nature shines through the cat's eyes.
Briseann an dúchas trí shúile an chait. [U]

HENS, GEESE AND DUCKS

Where you see shells you may guess eggs.
Thomhaisfeá uibheacha san áit a bhfeicfeá blaoscracha. [C]

•

It is a bad hen can't scrape for herself.
Is olc an chearc nach scríobann di féin. [U]

•

A laying hen is better than a nest of eggs.

•

The sitting hen never fattens.
Níor ramhraigh cearc ghoir riamh. [M]

•

The wisest hen at all lays out at times.

•

Though the hen may lay out her eggs will be found.

•

You can't expect a big egg from a little hen.

•

It is not the hen that cackles most lays the largest egg.

•

A dead hen is done laying.

The cocks crow but the hens deliver the goods.

•

Every cock can crow on his own dunghill.
Is teann gach coileach ar a charn aoiligh féin. [C]

•

A dead cock never crew.

•

If you want to keep up the stock keep an old gander and a young cock.

•

"You are welcome out," as Pára Bán said to the gosling.
[Pára Bán is a personal name, Pára being a diminutive of Pádraig.]

•

Those who have a goose will get a goose.

•

Send a goose to Hanover and she will come back a goose over.
Má chuireann tú gé go dtí an domhan teas, ní bheidh sí ina gandal ag teacht ar ais. [C]

•

Don't pluck your goose until you catch her.
Ná beannaigh an t-iasc go dtiocfaidh sé i dtír. [U]

•

"Time enough" lost the ducks and easy walking got them.
"Am go leor" a chaill na tonnóga. [U]
"Time enough" lost the duck but patience brought her home.

•

It's natural for ducks to go barefoot.
Sé dúchas na lachan snámh. [C]

BEES

Bee-keeping on farms, traditionally in conical straw skeps, was once much commoner than today. Lore about bees included informing them if there was a death in the household.

A rambling bee brings home the honey.
Ní chruinníonn cloch reatha caonach, ach cruinníonn meach siúil mil. [C]

•

Old bees yield no honey.

•

A small bee makes a cow gad.
Is minic a bhain creabhar preab as capall. [C]

CULTIVATION

The shortcut to food but the long way to work.
An cóngar chun an bhídh is an timpeall chun na hoibre. [M]

•

Every beginning is weak.
Bíonn gach tosnú lag. [M]

•

The man that waits for a good day will get it.
An té fhanas le lá breá gheobhaidh sé é. [U]

•

A farmer's work is never done.
Ní bheidh obair an talmhaí déanta go brách. [C]

•

From the king to the beggar they all depend on the farmer.

•

A good eye is worth two pairs of hands.
Is mó obair a níos súile an mháistir ná a chuid lámh. [C]

•

He who is a bad servant for himself is often a good servant
for others.
*An té bhíos ina dhrochsheirbhíseach dhó féin, is minic a bhíos
sé ina sheirbhíseach mhaith do dhaoine eile.* [C]

A backward man never prospers.
Ní gnáthach fear náireach éadálach. [M]

•

Work is better than talk.
Is fearr obair ná caint. [U]

•

Work while the bit is in your belly.

•

The four worst things:
ploughing in frost,
harrowing in rain,
making a ditch in summer
and building a wall in winter.
[Ditch, in this case, means a raised boundary.]
Treabhadh seaca is fuirseadh báistí, an dá rud is measa dhon talamh. [C]

•

It is not the day you are harrowing you should feed your horse.
Ní hé lá na báistí lá an phortaigh. [C]

•

The grass-harrow gathers no stones.

•

Harrowing is no good without cross-harrowing.

•

Have the supper ready when the harrow comes home.

•

You should never stop the plough to kill a mouse.

•

Seed must be saved before it's sown.

If you don't sow in the spring you will not reap in the autumn.

An té nach gcuireann san earrach, cha bhaineann sé san fhómhar. [U]

●

The seed you will sow is the corn you will reap.

Plant poacheens and you'll dig poacheens.

[Poacheens are small potatoes.]

Má chuireann tú póiríní bainfidh tú póiríní. [C]

●

More grows in a tilled field than is sowed in it.

●

Thistle seeds fly.

APPLES AND ORCHARDS

No use in throwing apples into an orchard.

Ag caitheamh úll isteach san úllghort. [C]

Don't throw apples into an orchard or carry turf to a bog.

Ag tabhairt cnó dho choll. [C]

●

Many a rose-cheeked apple is rotten at the core.

Is minic a bhíos an t-úll dearg go holc ina chroí. [C]

●

The shakiest tree in the orchard is sometimes the last to fall.

Chan é an crann a bhíos i bhfad ag crith an chéad chrann a thitfeas. [U]

Little apples will grow big.
Tagann fata mór as póirín. [C]

•

When the apple is ripe it will fall.
Nuair a bheas an t-úll aibí titfidh sé. [U]

•

Don't wait for apples, gather your own windfalls.

•

One rotten apple rots a bagful.

•

Apples will grow again.
Fásfaidh úlla arís. [C]

• • •

When all things spoke the potato said "Set me warm, dig me warm, eat me warm, that's all I want".

•

Time will tell and frost will dry the praties.
[Praties are potatoes]
Neosaidh an aimsir. [C]

•

If the potato misses Ireland's beaten.

•

Slight my meadow—buy my hay.
Más beag ort an léana, ná ceannaigh an féar. [U]

•

Time used sharpening a scythe is not time wasted.
Ní moill faobhar ach is mór an mhoill a bheith gan é. [M]

A good farmer is known by his crops.

•

It is not the big farmers who reap all the harvest.
Ní hiad na fir mhóra a ghearras an fómhar uilig. [C]

•

It is hard to get a good hook for a bad harvest man.
Is doiligh corrán maith a fháil do dhrochbhuanaí. [U]

•

Wisps make a bundle.
Níonn brobh beart. [C]
Méadaíonn [nó bailíonn] brobh beart (agus do-níd birt stáca).
[M]*

•

"Time enough" never cut the barley.
Níor bhain loirgne breaca earraigh fómhar riamh. [M]*

•

The more you tramp the dunghill the more the dirt rises.
Is leithne bualtrach bó le seasamh uirthi. [C]

•

Sea-wrack on the strand never manures the land.

•

Put a mud turf on a dish and it will be a mud turf still.
[Mud turf—an inferior kind needing more work to produce and
not being as efficient a fuel as the more solid spade-cut turf.]

•

The tree remains but not so the hand that put it.
Maireann an crann, ach ní mhaireann an lámh a chuir é. [C]

AT THE MILL

The mill cannot grind with the water that is past.
Ní fhéadann na muilte meilt leis an uisce a chuaidh thart. [C]

•

If you can't turn the wind you must turn the mill sails.

•

All's grist that comes to the mill.

•

One sack one sample.

•

It is hard for an empty bag to stand its lone.
Is deacair dho mhála folamh seasamh díreach. [C]
A full sack won't bend.

•

The bag is brother to the sack.
Is deartháir don tsac an mála. [U]

The miller's pigs are fat but it wasn't all mouter they ate.
[Mouter was the portion of customers' grain that the miller kept
in payment. In folk tradition the miller has a bad reputation and
so the proverb implies that the miller was keeping more than his
due.]

*Bíonn muca na muilteoirí ramhar; má tá, is ag Dia atá a fhios
cé leis an mhin a d'ith siad.* [U]

•

If you don't want flour do not go into the mill.

*Murar maith leat do mhéar a ghearradh, ná cuir roimh an
chorrán é.* [U]

HUNTING
AND
FISHING

"So near and yet so far," says the man when the bird lit on his gun.

•

A flying bird is any man's shot.

•

The wise bird flies lowest.

•

A closed fist never caught a bird.
Char ghabh dorn druidte seabhac riamh. [U]

•

An old fox is shy of a trap.

•

"We hounds kill the hare," quoth the lap-dog.

•

Wee dogs start the hare but big ones catch her.
Cuirfidh an madadh beag an gearria ina shuí, ach caithfidh an madadh mór a ghabháil. [U]

•

At times the slow hound is lucky.
Is minic cú mall sona. [M]

It is hard to put a dog off his track.

•

It is hard to hunt the hare out of the bush it is not in.
Is doiligh an gearria a chur as an tomóg nach bhfuil sé ann. [U]

•

Nearly never killed the hare.
Ní dhéanann "gearr dhó" an gnó. [C]

•

First catch your hare and then cook it.
Ná maraigh an fia go bhfeicidh tú é. [C]
Ná haltaigh do bhia go mbeidh sé id mhála. [M]

•

Long runs the hare but she is caught at last.
Más gasta an gearria beirtear fá dheireadh air. [U]

•

Praise the sea but keep near land.
Mol an mhónaidh is seachain í; cáin an choill is tathaigh í. [U]

•

Don't make bold with the sea.
Ná déan dánaíocht ar an bhfarraige. [C]

•

Listen to the sound of the river and you will catch a trout.
Éist le tuile na habhann is gheobhaidh tú breac. [U]

•

When you're not fishing be mending the nets.

•

It's late to be mending your nets when the eels are in the river.
Fál an bhodaigh in éis an ghoirt a mhilleadh. [U]

It's a good sign of fish to see some in the nets.
[Used in retort to being asked something obvious.]

•

It's seldom a fish loses his life for his breakfast.
A herring never was caught for his belly.
Mo ghrá-sa an scadán nár cailleadh ariamh lena ghoile. [C]

•

A herring in the pan is worth twenty in the sea.
Is fearr an breac atá sa dorn ná an breac atá san abhainn. [C]

A trout in the ashes is better than a salmon in the water.
Is fearr breac sa phota ná bradán sa linn. [U]

•

Better is a small fish than an empty dish.
Is fearr aon fhata amháin ná lán pláta dhe chraicne. [C]

WOODS
AND
WELLS

Never be first in the bog or last in the wood.
Ná bí ar thús corraigh ná ar dheireadh coille. [U]

•

It is not the same way everyone goes to the bog.

•

If there is a way into the wood there is also a way out of
it.
Ní lia bealach chun na coille ná bealach lena fágáil. [C]

•

Don't crow till you're out of the woods.
Ná tóg callán mór go bhfaighe tú amach as an choill. [U]

•

There is no tree but has a branch rotten enough to burn.

You will find enough of brushna in every wood to burn it.
[Brushna (Irish *brosna*) means wood for kindling. This can be
used to imply that there is a skeleton in the cupboard of every
family.]
Tá a loscadh féin i ngach coill. [U]

•

Bend with the tree that will bend with you.
Crom leis an chraobh a chromas leat. [U]

If the rowan tree is tall even so it is bitter on top.
Cé gurb ard é an crann caorthainn, bíonn sé searbh ar a bharr.
[C]

•

Little by little the oak tree grows.

•

Don't expect a cherry tree from an acorn.

•

An apple can't grow on a crab tree.
Cha dtig ón driseog ach an sméar. [U]

•

The older the crab-tree the more crabs it bears.

•

Willows are weak but they bind other wood.

• • •

"One look before is better than two behind," as the man
said when he fell into the well.
*Is fearr aon fhéachaint amháin romhat ná dhá fhéachaint id
dhiaidh.* [M]

•

The deeper the well the better the water.

•

It's a pure spring that never runs dry.

•

If you break the ice it is easy lifting a bucket of water.

Cold water will scald a clart.
[A clart is a dirty, slovenly woman. The proverb was collected in
County Monaghan.]

•

Never throw out the dirty water until you get in the clean.
*Ná caith an t-uisce salach amach go dtabhra tú an t-uisce glan
isteach.* [U]

•

You never know the want of water till the well goes dry.
Chan fhuil meas ar an uisce go dtriomaítear an tobar. [U]

•

Shallow brooks are noisy.
Is é an t-uisce is éadoimhne is mó tormán. [U]

•

If you had the Shannon in hell you'd soon be a millionaire.

•

Hills far away are green but they often have sour bottoms.
[Sour means boggy and infertile.]
*Is glas iad na cnoic i bhfad uainn,
Más glasmhar iad, ní féarmhar.* [C]

WILDLIFE

"Sour grapes," says the fox when he couldn't catch the chicken.

•

"More beard than brains," as the fox said of the goat.
"Is faide do chuid féasóige ná do chuid intleachta," mar a dúirt an sionnach leis an ngabhar. [C]

•

The fox never found a better messenger than himself.
Chan fhuair an mada rua teachtaire riamh ab fhearr ná é féin.
[U]

•

The fox finds his own stink first.
Is é an madarua is túisce a fhaigheann boladh a bhroma féin.
[M]

•

"Up and at it again," as the hedgehog said to the hare.

•

The last kick of a dying rat is always the worst.

•

Very few flocks that some bird out of them does not soil its own nest.

Little by little the bird builds her nest.
Ina bheagán is ina bheagán, mar thug an cat an meascán. [C]
Beagán ar bheagán a d'ith an cat an scadán. [M]

•

A crow won't caw without cause.

•

You can't teach a swallow how to fly.
Cuir comhairle ar ghabhainn. [C]
Sin ag baint na tua as láimh an tsaoir. [U]
Ag múineadh a phaidreacha dhon tsagart agus iad ar fad aige féin. [C]

•

A sandlark can't attend two strands.
Cha dtig leis an ghobadán friotháil ar an dá thrá. [U]*

•

You can't check a snipe for having a long bill.
Cad é an bac le mála na scadán boladh scadáin a bheith air? [U]

•

A wild goose never lays a tame egg.

•

A swan would die with pride only for its black feet.

•

— Every little frog is great in his own bog.

•

You can't pluck a frog.

Seven herrings are a meal for a salmon.

Seacht scadán díol bradáin,

Seacht mbradán díol róin,

Seacht róin díol muice mara,

Seacht muca mara díol míl mhóir,

Seacht míl mhóra díol an cheannruáin chróin,

Seacht gceannruáin chrón díol an domhain mhóir. [C]

•

"Strength," said the scutty wren when she pulled the maggot out of the hole.

"Neart," arsa an dreoillín nuair thit sé ar a thóin ag tarraingt péiste as an talamh. [C]

•

One beetle knows another.

Aithníonn ciaróg ciaróg eile. [U]

•

It's often a cleg made a bullock f--t.

[A cleg is a horse-fly.]

Is minic a bhain cuileog léim as bulóg. [C]

•

Of small account is a fly till it gets into the eye.

Is beag le rá an chuileog nó go dté sí ins an tsúil. [C]

HIGHROADS
AND
BYROADS

"I see," says the blind man when he was directed on his way.
"Chím," arsa an dall.
"Thug tú t'éitheach," arsa an balbhán. [C]

•

Ditches have ears.
Bíonn cluasa ar na claíocha. [C]

•

Half a leap falls into the ditch.
An té ná fuil léim aige cuimlíodh sé a thóin den gclaí. [M]

•

Never cross the fields while you have the road to go.
Ná tréig an bóthar mór mar gheall ar an aicearra. [U]
Never take the byway when you have the highway.

•

Be the road straight or crooked the high road is the shortest.
Cam nó díreach an ród, is é an bealach mór an aichearra. [U]

•

A going foot will always light on something.
Gheibheann cos ar siúl rud éigin. [C]

A stirring foot always gets something even if it's only a thorn.

•

No thorn as bad as the one out of the clabar.

[Clabar (Irish *clábar*) means mud]

•

A thorn,
a hound's tooth,
a fool's word.

[These are held to be the three sharpest things.]
Fiacal con,
dealg láibe,
nó focal amadáin:
ná trí nithe is géire amuigh. [M]

•

Never praise a ford till you are over.
Molann gach duine an t-áth mar gheobhadh sé é. [C]

•

Leave the kesh as it is.

[A kesh is a man-made causeway across boggy ground. Kesh occurs frequently in place-names.]
Fág an Chéis [or *an cheist*] *mar tá sí.* [C]

•

"Who knows?" as the woman said when she followed the coach.

•

The loosest spoke in the wheel rattles most.
Is é an taobhlán is lofa is luaithe a níos gíoscarnach. [U]
The wheel that's weak is apt to creak.

"What a dust we kick up," as the fly said to the cart-wheel.
"Nach mise a thóg an dusta?" arsa an chuileog i ndiaidh an chóiste. [U]

•

An empty cart makes most noise.
Is é an carr folamh is mó a ní tormán. [U]

•

A car on the road earns money but two in the ditch earns nothing.

•

A rolling stone gathers no moss but it gets a great shine.
Cha chruinníonn cloch chasaidh caonach. [U]

•

The longest road has an end and the straightest road has an end.
Níl lá dhá fhad nach dtig a thráthnóna. [C]

•

Pains and patience would take a snail to America.
Aimsir agus foighid, bhéarfadh sé an seilide go hIarúsailéim. [U]

•

Two shorten the road.
Giorraíonn beirt bóthar. [C]

•

It is a long lane that has no turn.
Is fada an bóthar nach bhfuil casadh ann. [U]
It is a long road that has no public house!

MONEY
AND
MARKETS

"Well agra!" said Nancy Carr, "It's many's the crush the poor get."
[Agra (Irish *a ghrá*) is a term of endearment]

●

It is a poor village that has neither smoke nor fire.
Is baile bocht baile gan toit gan tine. [U]

●

→ The town leaves an empty pocket with people.

●

Nothing for nothing in Ballysadare.
A Sligo proverb; one similar came from Louth:
You'll get nothing for nothing in Ardee.

●

Money is like muck—no good till spread.

●

A wet day is a good one for changing a pound.

●

There's always money where there's dirt.

●

Money makes the horse gallop whether he has shoes or not.

Money would make the pot boil if you would throw ice in the fire.

•

A penny in a poor man's pocket is better than two pennies in a rich man's pocket.

•

One penny gets another.
Gheibh pingin pingin eile. [U]

•

You may not be talking of a penny when you have not a halfpenny.

•

Your pocket is your friend.
Is é do phóca do charaid. [U]

•

Your eye is your mark, your pocket is your friend, let the money be the last thing you'll part with.

•

Before you buy consult your purse.
Déan do mhargadh de réir do sparáin. [C]

•

Don't buy a purse with the last half-crown.

•

Never buy through your ears but through your eyes.

•

Taste and try before you buy.

•

You can never buy sweets for nothing.

It is hard to pay for a loaf when you have it eaten.
Dearmadtar an mhaith a déantar. [C]*

•

You can't have the hen and the price of her.
Ní fhéadfadh sé a bheith ina phic is ina mhála. [M]
An té itheas an bhulóg, ní bhíonn sí fana ascaill aige. [C]

•

The thing that is bought dear is often sold cheap.
An rud a cheannaítear go daor díoltar go saor é. [U]

•

There are good goods in small parcels and poison in some.
Bíonn earraí maithe i mbeairtíní beaga. [C]

•

Don't bring all your eggs to the one market.
Ná cuir do chuid uibheacha uilig in aon bhosca amháin. [C]

•

Monaghan Day pays for all.
[Monaghan Day was 25th February and one of the biggest local fairs in County Leitrim (where the proverb was collected) was held in Mohill on that day.]

•

If you have only a buck goat be in the middle of the fair with him.
Mura mbeadh agat ach pocán gabhair bí í lár an aonaigh leis.
[M]

•

There's no use in shouting in the fair when you have nothing to sell.

Ireland for a penny, but where is the penny?
Éirinn ar phingin; má tá, cá bhfuil an phingin? [U]

THE LAW

"Hame is hamely," as the devil said when he found himself in the lawcourt.

•

Don't go to law with the devil in the court of hell.
Ná téirigh chun dlí leis an diabhal 's an chúirt in ifreann. [C]

•

If you go to court leave your soul at home.

•

A word in the court is worth a pound in the purse.
Is fearr focal sa chúirt ná punt sa sparán. [M]
A good friend in court is better than money in the purse.
Is fearr cara sa chúirt ná bonn sa sparán. [U]

•

A pennyworth of law is enough for anyone.

•

Law is costly; shake hands and be friends.

•

Lawyers' houses are made of fools' heads.

•

A lawmaker is a law-breaker.
Lucht déanamh dlí, chan cóir dóibh bheith a' briseadh dlí. [U]

The law is no respecter of persons.

•

Possession is eleven points of the law.
Ponc den dlí an tseilbh. [M]

•

New kings make new laws.

FRIENDS
AND
NEIGHBOURS

A man is known by his company.
Aithnítear duine ar a chuideachta. [C]

•

As you live yourself you judge your neighbour.
Mar chaitheas duine a bheatha, tabhair breith ar a chomharsain.
[C]

•

There is more friendship in a half of whiskey than in a
churn of buttermilk.
*Is mó an carthanas a bhíos i ngloine biotáille ná bhíos i mbairille
bláthaí.* [C]

•

Friends are like fiddle-strings and they must not be screwed
too tightly.

•

Don't be hard and don't be soft and don't desert your
friend for your own share.
Ná bí cruaidh agus ná bí bog; ná tréig do charaid ar do chuid.
[C]

It is a pity on a man that is content in the troubles of his neighbours.
Is mairg a fhaigheann sólás i ndólás a chomharsan. [M]

•

Now I have a cow and a horse and everyone bids me good-morrow.

•

Keep in with a bad person for a good person will never do you any harm.
Coinnigh an drochdhuine leat, is ní dhéanfaidh an duine maith dochar duit. [U]

•

Don't break your shins off your neighbour's pots.

•

Don't outstay your welcome like a neighbour's goat.
Cuairt ghearr is imeacht buíoch. [C]*
Cuairt gan fuílleach. [C]*

•

Come seldom, come welcome.
Ná téigh ach go hannamh go tigh do charad is gheobhair fáilte.
[Téigh ann go minic is beidh romhat deargchnáide]. [M]
Ní bhíonn fáilte roimh minic a thig. [C]

•

Everyone is nice till the cow gets into the garden.
Bíonn gach duine lách go dtéann bó ina gharraí. [M]

•

Good mearings make good neighbours.
[A mearing is a boundary between land owned by different people.]
Fál maith a dhéanas comharsana maithe. [C]

— 90 —

If you want to know me come and live with me.

Níl eolas gan aontíos. [U]

Everybody is sweet to your face until you burn a stack of turf with them.

Tá chuile duine lách go gcaitear mála salainn leis. [C]

•

Never want while your neighbour has it.

•

You can live without your own but not without your neighbour.

Tig leat déanamh gan do dhaoine féin; má tá, cha dtig leat déanamh gan comharsana. [U]

You have your neighbour when your friends are far away.

[In this and the following proverb the word friend is used in the sense of relation. The first is from Cavan and the second from Leitrim.]

Your neighbour is your friend.

[The nearest to you when you need help.]

•

Más fada uait do dhuine féin, is fearr dhuit do chomharsa. [C]

•

If you have not your neighbour you have nobody.

•

Don't take a slate off your own house to put on your neighbour's.

Ná bain tuí de do thoigh féin le sclátaí a chur ar thoigh fir eile. [U]

If two neighbours want to fight they will find a quarrel in
a straw.
Char fhadaigh dís tine gan troid. [U]*

•

Strife is better than loneliness.
Is fearr imreas ná uaigneas. [C]

•

The war of friends doesn't last long.
Ní buan cogadh na gcarad. [C]

•

Never go between the skin and the tree.
Ná bí ag dul idir an craiceann is an crann. [U]

•

Kick him again, he's no relation.

SPORT
AND
PASTIMES

One tale is good till another is told.
Is maith scéal go dtig scéal eile. [U]

•

One story brings on another.
Scéal a tharraingeas scéal. [C]

•

Never fly your kite too high.

•

The best swimmer is on the bank.
Is maith an snámhadóir a bhíos ar an mbóthar. [C]
He is a good hurler who sits on the ditch.
Is maith an t-iománaí an té a bhíonn ar an gclaí. [M]
The best footballer is always on the ditch.
Is maith an báireoir a bhíos ar an gclaí. [C]
The man on the grass is a good rider.
Is maith an marcach, an fear bhíos ar an talamh. [C]

•

It's hard to make a hunter out of an ass.

•

A cart-horse could never win the Derby.

The world wouldn't make a race-horse of an ass.
Ní dhéanfadh an saol capall ráis d'asal. [M]

•

The morning of the race is not the morning to feed your horse.
Tá sé rómhall croisín a chur faoi theach nuair a thiteas sé. [U]*

•

The race-horse throws his heels the highest.

•

The best horse doesn't always win the race.
Is minic nach é an capall is fearr a thóigeas an rása. [C}

•

The lighter the jockey the swifter the horse goes.

•

"Diamonds for life," said the cardplayer's wife.

•

Cards and decks the devil's vice and jackstones worse than all.

•

Spades for the bog.

•

One good trick is better than twenty bad ones.
Is fearr cleas maith ná fiche droch-chleas. [C]

•

Fair play is bonny play.
Fair play Chúige Uladh, triúr ar an bhfear! [C]

•

The best throw of a dice is to throw it away.

It is hard to get a good book for a bad reader.

A pun on the long established:

It is hard to get a good hook for a bad reaper.

•

Bad books are bad companions.

•

Dancing was first started by a madman.

•

Slips belong to dancing.

[A slip in a dance is a gliding step used, for instance, in the slip jig.]

•

Company brings the dogs to dance and night brings home the crows.

Préachán an tráthnóna. [M]

CHURCH
AND
CLERGY

The nearer the church the further from God.
An té is giorra dhon teampall, ní hé is giorra dhon altóir. [C]

●

All are not saints that go to church.

●

A big church and small devotions.

●

Forced prayers no devotion.

●

A good turn in the kitchen is as good as a prayer in the chapel.

●

Don't be too friendly with the clergy and don't fall out with them.
Ná bí róbheag is ná bí rómhór leis an gcléir. [M]
Don't be in or out with the priests.
Ná bí mór ná beag le sagart. [C]

Put the priest in the middle of the parish.
[This refers to the former custom of putting a basket of boiled potatoes (the "priest") on a pot in the middle of the floor. The potatoes were then eaten directly from it by those sitting round.]

A dumb priest never gets a parish.
Ní fhaigheann sagart balbh beatha. [M]

•

It is a poor priest that has no curate.
Is bocht an sagart nach mbíonn cléireach aige. [U]

•

The habit does not make the monk.

•

Patience and perseverance made a bishop of his reverence.
Patience and perseverance won a wife for his reverence.
Faigheann bád foireann is muirín ba. [C]*

•

The minister christens his own child first.
Baisteann an sagart a pháiste féin a chéaduair. [U]

•

A Sabbath well spent brings a week of content.

OCCUPATIONS

"Anything to bother the hunger," like the tailor when he swallowed the midge.

"Rud ar bith leis an ocras a bhodhradh," agus é ag ithe míoltóige.
[C]

•

He that has a trade has an estate.

An té a mbíonn ceird aige, bíonn beatha aige. [C]

•

A good tradesman has all his tools.

•

A carpenter is known by his chips.

•

Though the carpenter is bad the splinter is good.

Más olc an saor is maith an scealbóg. [U]

•

Old masons make good barrowmen.

•

A bad cobbler will never make a shoemaker.

•

If you knew everything you could be a doctor.

Charity covers a multitude of sins, but a tailor covers a multitude of sinners.

•

Never judge cloth by tailors' words.

•

Marry a tailor and you marry a thimble.

•

It would take nine tailors to hoist a bag of dust on a sow.
Ní bhíonn ins gach táilliúir ach an deichiú cuid d'fhear. [C]*

•

A tailor is known by his clippings.

•

A lazy tailor has always a long thread.
Snáithe fhada an táilliúir fhalsa. [U]

•

No odds among tinkers who carries the budget.
[A buget is a beggar's bag]

•

A tinker's wife and a tailor's wife are the two that never agree.
Bean táilliúra nó bean tincéara—sin beirt bhan ná réann le chéile. [M]

•

Everything goes in the beggar's bag.

•

It's a poor beggar that can't shun one door.
Is olc an bacach nach dtig leis toigh amháin a seachnadh. [U]

•

Carry a beggarman seven years, leave him down once and you never carried him at all.

When it is raining porridge the beggars have no spoons.

•

Beg from a beggar and you'll never be rich.
Bí ag iarratas ar dhuine bhocht, is ní bhfaighidh tú do shaibhreas a choíchin uaidh. [C]

•

Put a beggar on horseback and he'll ride to Cork.
Cuir bacach ar dhroim gearráin is rachaidh sé ar cos in airde. [U]

•

The thief is no danger to a beggar.
Ní baol don mbacach an gadaí. [U]

•

Mór keeps herself and her maid looking for alms.
Cailín ag Mór is Mór ag iarraidh déirce. [C]
[Mór is a woman's name which is often used in proverbs.]

CLOTHES
AND
APPEARANCE

"Nothing like a change of linen," as the old woman said when she turned her shift.
"Is deas an rud an ghlaine," mar a dúirt an bhean nuair a thiontaigh sí a léine i ndiaidh seacht mbliana. [U]

•

Beauty is only skin deep, ugliness goes to the bone.
Ní théann áilleacht thar an gcraiceann. [C]

•

Beauty never boiled the pot and ugliness never thickened it.
Cha chuireann maise an pota ar gail. [U]

•

What is beauty to comfort?

•

An inch is a great deal on a nose.
Is mór orlach de shrón duine. [U]

•

A crowl on a creepie looks nothing.
[Collected in County Cavan. A crowl here probably means an undersized person or child and a creepie is a stool.]

•

Every fault is a fashion.

You might as well be out of the world as out of the fashion.
*Bheadh sé chomh maith agat bheith as an tsaol is bheith as an
fhaisiún.* [U]

•

When a man's coat is threadbare it is easy to pick a hole
in it.

•

Many an honest heart beats under a ragged coat.
Is minic a bhí croí fíor fá chasóg stróicthe. [C]

•

A good coat covers a lot of rags.

•

Stitch by stitch the suit is made.
Líontar sac le póiríní. [C]
Is mór iad na beaganna i dteannta a chéile. [M]*

•

It's hard to tear a stocking across.

•

A coat twice turned is not worth sleeving.

•

A patch is better than a hole, but devil in it but that.
Is fearr paiste ná poll,
Is fearr lom ná léan,
Is fearr maol ná bheith gan ceann
Is diabhal ann ach sin féin. [U]

•

Patch beside patch is neighbourly but patch upon patch is
beggarly.

Clothes make the man.
Is é an t-éadach a ní an duine. [U]

•

You cannot tell from a man's clothes how much he is making but you must look at his wife's.

•

The shoemaker's wife and the blacksmith's horse often go unshod.
Is minic drochbhróga ar bhean gréasaí. [C]
Ba mhinic drochbhríste ar tháilliúir is drochbhróga ar ghréasaí. [C]

•

He is no poor man that has two shirts.

•

It's a small smitch that spoils a Sunday shirt.
[Collected in County Monaghan where the meaning of smitch was given as "dirty spot."]
Is beag an rud a shalódh stocaí bána. [C]
Dá ghile an t-éadach is fusa é a shalachadh. [M]*

•

Many a white collar covers a dirty neck.

•

The life of an old hat is to cock it, of an old shoe to black it.

•

When your hat is on your house is thatched.

•

Ill got, ill gone, like the old woman's bonnet.
An rud a gheibhtear go holc, téann sé go holc. [U]

Fancy buys the ribbon but taste ties the bow.

•

You cannot take a glove off the hand that it is not on.

•

Pride without profit wearing gloves and going barefooted.

•

A ring on the finger and not a stitch of clothes on the back.

•

Nan's dressed up and the wardrobe empty.

•

Silks and satins, scarlet and velvet often put out the kitchen fire.

•

If you don't give me charity don't tear my coat.
Ach mura dtabhara tú dada dom, ná stróc mo mhála. [U]

•

When you give away your old breeches don't cut the buttons off.
Má thugann tú iasacht do chuid brístí, ná gearr na cnaipí díobh. [U]
It's no use giving an old pair of trousers if you pull the seat out of them.

•

You cannot take the britches off a Highlander.
Is doiligh stocaí a bhaint d'fhear coslomnocht. [U]

God's leather to God's weather.
[A comment collected with this proverb was that children should be allowed to go barefooted summer and winter.]

It is all the same to the man with the brogues where he puts his foot.
Is cuma le fear na mbróg cá gcuireann sé a chos. [M]

•

The beauty of an old shoe is to polish it.
Seanbhróg smeartha bróg nua. [M]
Cuireann búcla slacht ar sheanbhróig. [C]*

•

Every man knows where the boot hurts him.
Is ag duine féin is fearr a fhios cén áit a luíonn a bhróg air. [U]

•

Bad shoes are better than none.
Aon tsúil amháin i gceann, is fearr ná bheith gan aon tsúil. [C]

•

Never throw away the old boots till you get new ones.
Ná caith uait an tseanbhróg nó go bhfaighidh tú an bhróg nua. [C]

•

Any fool carries an umbrella on a wet day but the wise man carries it every day.
Béarfaidh an fear críonna a chóta leis lá tirim. [U]

MARRIAGE

"Better marry than burn," as Saint Paul said.

•

It is a lonesome washing without a man's shirt in it.
Is uaigneach an níochán nach mbíonn léine ann. [U]

•

Court abroad but marry at home.
Iarr i bhfad uait ach pós i ngar dhuit. [C]

•

The oftener the blanket is doubled the warmer.
Is teoide don mbrat a dhúbladh. [U]

•

Love the dunghill and you'll see no motes in it.
Má ghráíonn tú an t-aoileach ní fheicfidh tú drugann ann. [U]

•

He who dotes in the dark sees no motes.

Three things you cannot comprehend:
the mind of a woman,
the working of the bees
and the ebb and flow of the tide.
Na trí nithe is deacra a thuiscint:
intleacht na mban,
obair na mbeach,
tuile is trá na mara. [C]

•

There are matches for ciarogs.
[Ciarog (Irish *ciaróg*) is a kind of beetle]
Fáigheann ciaróg ciaróg eile amach. [C]

•

There is never an old brogue but there is a foot to fit it.
Níl aon tseanstoca ná faigheann seanbhróg. [M]

•

Fits find each other.

•

Don't be too sure of your match like O'Foy.
Ná bí róchinnte. [C]
Sé an chaoi is fearr, gan a bheith róchinnte. [C]*

•

It is better to be refused for a hook on a harvest day than
to be refused for a wife.

•

Marry a mountain woman and you will marry the
mountain.
Pós bean tsléibhe is pósfaidh tú an sliabh uilig. [U]

Marry a woman from Truagh and you marry all Truagh
[Truagh is Monaghan's smallest barony.]
Pós bean ó Bhéara is pósfair Béara go léir. [M]

•

"That'll be the end of us all," as the old maid said when
she saw the wedding.

•

Poor people must have poor weddings.

•

What is bound in harvest will be loosened in spring.
[Long ago the common time for weddings was in spring during
the weeks prior to Lent. Marriage in autumn would not have
been encouraged as there was little time to spare at the all
important harvest period. The metaphor is taken from binding
the sheaves at harvest and loosening them later for threshing.]

•

There's no cure for love but marriage.
Níl leigheas ar an ngrá ach an pósadh. [C]

•

There is no feast till a roast and no torment till a marriage.
Ní céasta go pósta is ní féasta go róstadh. [M]

•

It's all better than a bad marriage.

HEALTH

A glutton lives to eat, a wise man eats to live.

•

Diet cures more than the doctor.

•

Better pay the cook than the doctor.

•

Sleep is better than medicine.

•

The beginning of health is sleep, the end of it is a sigh.
Tosach loinge clár,
Tosach átha clocha,
Tosach flaithe fáilte,
Tosach sláinte codladh.
Deireadh loinge í a bhá,
Deireadh átha loscadh,
Deireadh flaithe cáineadh
Is deireadh sláinte osna. [M]

•

A sick man reported dead always recovers.

•

A dying rannie often lives longer than a sound man.
[In Scots—rennie or ronnie means a constant complainer.]

A good laugh and a long sleep are the two best cures in the doctor's book.
Gáire maith is codladh fada—an dá leigheas is fearr i leabhar an dochtúra. [U]

•

A good laugh is as good as a day at the seaside.

•

A day in the country is worth a month in the town.

•

What butter or whiskey will not cure is incurable.
An rud nach leigheasann im ná uisce beatha, níl leigheas air. [U]

•

Whiskey when you're sick makes you well, whiskey makes you sick when you're well.

•

Doctors differ and patients die.

•

A light heart lives long.
Maireann croí éadrom i bhfad. [C]

•

A heavy heart seldom combs a grey head.
Cha chíorann tú ceann liath choíche. [U]

Three places to be avoided:
a doctor's door,
a priest's door
and a barrack door.
Gob ó aturnae,
gob ó dhochtúir,
gob corr scréachóg. [C]

●

Every cripple has his own way of walking.

DEATH

Never say die while there is meat on the shin of a wren.

•

You're late to run for the priest when the person is dead.
Chan é an t-am a dhul fán dochtúir nuair atá an duine marbh.
[U]

•

Death and marriages make changes.
Éag is imirce a chloíos tíobhas. [U]

•

Every day is a day nearer the grave.

•

Death takes the young as well as the old.
Níl fhios cé is luaithe, bás an tseanduine ná bás an duine óig.
[C]*

•

Death never gives a year's warning to anyone.

•

Death comes like a thief in the night.
Tigeann an bás mar ghadaí san oíche. [C]

•

There is hope from the sea but no hope from the cemetery.
Bíonn súil le muir, ach cha bhíonn súil le cill. [U]

- There is no cure or help against death.
  Chan fhuil lia ná leigheas ar an bhás. [U]

  •

- Death is the poor man's doctor.
  'Sé an bás leigheas an duine bhoicht. [C]
  Lia gach boicht bás. [M]

  •

Death does not come without a reason.
Cha dtig an t-éag gan ceannfháth. [U]

  •

What you think is worse than your death is perhaps for your good.
An rud is measa leat ná an bás, is leas dhuit go minic é. [U]

  •

A wise man never saw a dead man.
Ní fhaca duine críonna duine marbh. [C]

  •

It is easy to pass by a dead man's door.
Is furaist gabháil thar dhoras duine mhairbh nuair ná bíonn sé féin ná a mhadra istigh. [M]

  •

It is easy to rob a dead man's house.

  •

Sudden death, sudden mercy.

LUCK

Luck's a king and luck's a beggar.

•

Luck and laziness go hand in hand.
Is minic a bhíos rath ar rapladh. [U]

•

There is luck in leisure.

•

Good luck beats early rising.
Is fearr an t-ádh maith ná éirí go moch. [U]

Better to be fortunate than rich.
Is fearr sona ná saibhir. [U]

•

It's better to be lucky than wise.
Is fearr a bheith sona ná críonna. [U]

•

'Tis the fool has luck.
Bíonn ádh ar amadán. [U]

•

Perseverance is the mother of good luck.

There is no luck where there is no correction.
Ní bhíonn an rath ach mar a mbíonn an smacht. [M]
Bad luck never comes its lone.
Ní tháinig trioblóid riamh ina haonar. [M]

•

Dick died and the hen laid out.
*"Ní thig an léan leis féin," mar dúirt an tseanbhean, nuair
cailleadh a fear 's rug an chearc amuigh.* [C]

•

Good care takes the head off bad luck.
Baineann an coimhéad maith an ceann den tubaiste. [U]
Briseann an t-aireachas muineál an mhí-ádha. [C]

•

The worse luck now the better again.

•

When luck comes it come in a bucketful.
*Nuair a bhíonns sé againn bíonn sé againn go tiubh, is nuair
a bhíonn muid folamh bímid folamh go dubh.* [U]*

THE SUPERNATURAL

Speak to the devil and you'll hear the clatter of his hooves.
Trácht ar an diabhal agus taispeánfaidh sé é féin. [U]

•

It's time enough to shake hands with the devil when you meet him.
Ná beannaigh don diabhal go mbuaileann tú leis. [C]

•

Pulling the devil by the leg is a bad grip.
Ag tarraingt an diabhail de ghreim eireabaill. [C]

•

It is easy preaching to the devil with a full stomach.

•

What comes in on the devil's back goes out on his horns.
An rud a fhaightear de dhroim an diabhail imíonn sé faoina bholg. [M]

•

The devil will have his own.

•

It is a rocky road to heaven.

•

A good heart never went to hell.
Níor chuaigh fial riamh go hifreann. [M]

— There's favour in hell and the biggest devil gets it.
Tá fábhar in ifreann. [C]

•

Banagher bangs the devil.
[Because of this and a similar expression the name is known far and wide. Therer are several Banaghers, each, no doubt, identifying with the saying.]

•

It's hard to kill a bad thing.
Is doiligh drochrud a mharú. [C]

•

The devil couldn't kill a bad thing.

•

A chance shot may kill the devil.

•

When God comes in the door the devil flies out of the window.

•

God's help is nearer than the door.
Is foisce cabhair Dé ná an doras. [U]

•

God is good till morning.
Is maith Dia go lá. [U]

•

The Lord never closed one door but He opened another.
Níor dhún Dia doras riamh nach bhfosclódh Sé ceann eile. [C]
God never shut a gap but He opened another one.
Níor dhún Dia bearna riamh ná go n-osclódh Sé ceann eile. [M]
God never wets anything but He dries it again.

The People
Who Drank
Water from the
River

by

James Kennedy

A memorable evocation of a bygone era in rural
Ireland

POOLBEG

Land of Milk and Honey

The Story of Traditional Irish Food and Drink

by

Bríd Mahon

With an introduction and recipes by
Kathleen Watkins

POOLBEG

School for Hope

by
Michael McLaverty

A novel of love, guilt, fear and forgiveness

POOLBEG